curry lovers

curry lovers

FROM KERALAN FISH CURRY TO KOFTAS IN CINNAMON MASALA

ROOPA GULATI

with photography by RICHARD JUNG

jacqui small

First published in 2007 by Jacqui Small,
an imprint of Aurum Press,
7 Greenland Street, London NW1 0ND

Publisher   Jacqui Small
Editor   Nicola Graimes
Art Director   Ashley Western
Food stylist   Jayne Cross
Props stylist Roisin Nield
Production   Peter Colley

A catalogue record for this book is
available from the British Library.

ISBN-10: 1 903221 94 3
ISBN-13: 978 1 903221 94 5

2010   2009   2008   2007   2006

10 9 8 7 6 5 4 3 2 1

Printed and bound in China

Half title page, Pork Vindaloo, see page 35.
Title page, from left to right,
Shrimp in Tamarind Sauce, see page 47;
Potatoes with Cumin, see page 50;
Ginger Beef Curry with Poppy Seeds, see page 32;
and Tarka Dal, see page 58.
Contents page, Cabbage Thoran, see page 53.

contents

introduction

These days you can walk into any supermarket and buy an "Indian" ready-meal; hopefully I'll inspire you to think otherwise. Indian cooking doesn't have to be a grind, it's about enjoying the real — the aroma of spices toasting; the flavour of freshly ground garam masala; the homely appeal of dishes cooked from scratch. From street snacks to palace feasts, this is a book about making marvellous meals and bringing family and friends to the table.

ROOPA GULATI

boiled rice

The lightness and fluffiness of basmati rice cooked in a big pan of boiling water is unrivalled. Follow a few foolproof points and you'll get it right every time.

1 For 4–5 people, rinse 400g (2 cups) basmati rice in cold running water. Put the rice into a bowl, pour over cold water to cover, and leave to soak for 15 minutes.

2 Bring a large pan of salted water to the boil. Add the drained rice and cook over a medium heat for 5–7 minutes, until tender.

3 Tip the rice into a colander, drain off the water, and serve (if you're not going to eat the rice straight away, run warm water through the hot rice for a few moments — this helps to get rid of any excess starch).

Variations on plain boiled rice:

1 Soak a generous pinch of saffron strands in 30ml (2 tbsp) warm water. Set aside for 1 hour until the water turns auburn. Drizzle the saffron and its soaking liquid over freshly boiled rice and fork through.

2 Heat 30ml (2 tbsp) vegetable oil in a small pan and add 2 tsp cumin seeds. Swirl the cumin around for about 30 seconds until it darkens and gives off a nutty aroma. Pour the cumin and oil over hot boiled rice and gently mix in.

3 To add flavour to cooked rice, add 4 cardamom, 4 cloves, 1 cinnamon stick, and 2 bay leaves to the cooking water.

garam masala

I've been using this recipe for over 30 years — there's no comparison between home-ground spice mixes and shop-bought ones.

20g brown cardamom seeds, pods discarded
20g cinnamon stick, broken into pieces
20g black peppercorns
3 heaped tsp cumin seeds
2 blades mace
2 tsp cloves
$^1/_2$ tsp grated nutmeg

1 Tip the spices into a coffee grinder and process until finely ground. Sift the spices and store in a lidded jam jar (the spice mix will keep for about 2 months, or freeze in an airtight plastic box for 6–8 months).

naan

My mother would make her own naan bread, leaving the dough to rise in the airing cupboard — covered with her least-loved tea towel. They tasted as good as the ones you find in downtown Delhi.

500g (5 cups) plain (all-purpose) flour
1 tsp salt
$^1/_4$ tsp baking powder

2 tsp instant (active) dry yeast
2 tsp caster (superfine) sugar
75g (6 tbsp) softened butter
150ml ($^2/_3$ cup) warm milk
125ml ($^1/_2$ cup) plain yoghurt

Topping:
15g (1 tbsp) butter, melted
1 tsp nigella seeds

1 Sift the flour, salt, and baking powder into a bowl and stir in the yeast and sugar. Rub the butter in with your fingertips until the mixture resembles coarse crumbs.

2 Combine the milk and yoghurt in a jug and gradually add to the flour. Using your hands, bring everything together into a soft dough. Turn out onto a floured surface and knead until smooth.

3 Transfer the dough to a lightly oiled bowl, cover loosely with plastic wrap then leave for about 1 hour in a warm place, until doubled in size.

4 Punch the dough down and leave to rise again until doubled in size (it should feel springy to the touch). Divide the dough into 12 even-sized pieces and shape into balls. Cover with a cloth while you cook the naan.

5 Heat a griddle over a medium heat and preheat the grill. Roll out one of the dough balls into an elongated oval, about 5mm ($^1/_4$in) thick. Griddle the bread over a gentle heat until golden on one side.

6 Transfer the bread to a baking (cookie) sheet — its uncooked side facing upwards. Brush the top with melted butter and sprinkle with nigella seeds. Pop the naan under a hot grill for a minute or so until golden. Repeat with the remaining dough.

basic ingredients

GHEE
Available from Asian stores, ghee is clarified butter made from buffalo' or cow's milk. Many modern cooks use vegetable oil as a healthier alternative.

TAMARIND
This dark fruit is prized for its tangy flavour and can be bought fresh in its pod, dried in compressed cakes, or as a concentrated paste.

COCONUT
The mainstay of South Indian cooking, coconut milk enriches masalas, and the versatile white kernel is often incorporated in auspicious sweetmeats, chutneys, and curry pastes.

CORIANDER (CILANTRO)
Notable for its astringent, citrus-like flavour, coriander (cilantro) is the most widely used herb in Asian cooking. The stems have a more pronounced flavour than the leaves.

GREEN MANGO
Firm to the touch, green mangoes are extremely tart, but sweeten up a treat after being cooked with sugar – perfect for chutneys and relishes.

CURRY LEAVES
A key seasoning in dishes from the southern and western coastal states, the zesty flavour of curry leaves is enhanced when fried in hot oil.

GARLIC
An integral ingredient in Punjabi dishes, garlic is often married with ginger and used in meaty marinades, onion-based masalas, and as a tempering for dals.

GINGER
Popular across South Asia, ginger root is usually used fresh rather than in its dried powdered form; remember to pare the thin beige skin before using.

YOGHURT
Home cooks in India tend to make their own yoghurt. Well-suited as a cooling accompaniment to spicy main dishes, it's also used in curries, marinades, and cooling drinks like lassi.

JAGGERY
Made from sugar cane, jaggery has a crumbly texture and a notable caramel-like flavour. It's often paired with tamarind when making sweet-sour chutneys and curry sauces.

FRESH CHILLIES
A wide variety of chillies are used in cooking and they come in varying sizes and strengths. For a milder flavour, remove the seeds and membrane.

LENTILS & PULSES
Affordable and nutritious, lentils and pulses are valuable staples for everyday meals. When finely ground to a flour, they are also used in batters, pancakes, and Indian sweetmeats.

SPICES

GREEN & BROWN CARDAMOM
Brown cardamom pods are strong in flavour, adding a nuttiness to robust curries and garam masalas, while green cardamoms have a sweeter character that is best suited to mild and fragrant dishes.

FENNEL SEEDS
The seeds are prized for their anise-like flavour and work well with ginger in masalas and pickles. They're also enjoyed as a digestive after meals.

CUMIN SEEDS
Toasted and ground cumin seeds are a natural match with yoghurt dishes. Whole seeds, when fried in oil, add depth to pan-Indian curries, dals, and vegetable dishes.

MUSTARD SEEDS
In southern and western coastal states, black mustard seeds are popped in hot oil and used to temper dishes, while in Bengal, seeds are often pounded and added to pungent masalas.

TURMERIC
In its dried, powdered form turmeric is an everyday spice that lends a pale orange hue and peppery flavour to curries, dals, vegetable dishes, and fragrant pickles.

DRIED CHILLIES
Available in varying sizes and strengths, dried red chillies are either soaked in water before using, or fried in hot oil to release their heat.

CORIANDER SEEDS
A popular spice throughout India, coriander seeds are dry roasted before being ground to a powder. They have a pronounced 'woody' aroma and slightly sweet flavour.

CLOVES
A key component of garam masala, cloves have a richly intense character, and when used sparingly, are a popular infusion spice for rice dishes and meaty curries.

CASSIA
Often interchangeable with cinnamon, cassia is most often used in Indian cooking as a seasoning, and has a fuller flavour than the more delicately scented cinnamon.

NUTMEG & MACE
Mace is the wispy, basket-like cover that cradles the nutmeg seed. Although both spices have a warm, nutty flavour, mace is prized for its subtle flavour.

MANGO POWDER
Made from the dried, unripe fruit, beige-hued mango powder adds a tart tang to curries and is sometimes sprinkled over North Indian snacks, salads, and tandoori grills.

CAROM SEEDS
Better known as 'ajwain', these small, oval-shaped seeds have a strong thyme-like flavour that works well with fish marinades, Gujarati vegetarian dishes, and crisp-fried snacks.

salads & chutneys

crisp salad with cumin and lime dressing

The chill of a lime-drenched salad is a permanent feature on Indian tables, especially during the scorching heat of an Indian summer. A crisp contrast to robust curries, this salad also makes a fabulous relish for meaty kebabs and grills.

SERVES 4

1/2 cucumber, diced
3 tomatoes, seeded and diced
4 spring onions (scallions), finely sliced
1 red apple, cored and diced
juice of 1 lime
1/2 tsp cumin seeds, toasted and ground
1 red chilli, seeded and finely chopped
1/4 tsp coarsely ground black peppercorns
2 tbsp fresh coriander (cilantro) leaves

1 Combine the cucumber, tomatoes, spring onions (scallions), and apple in a bowl.

2 To make the dressing, whisk together the lime juice, cumin powder, red chilli, and ground pepper. Pour the dressing over the salad, mix well until combined and serve sprinkled with fresh coriander (cilantro).

(Pictured previous page)

great idea – we added spring greens and oil + honey to dressing

potato salad with date and tamarind chutney

After my parents moved to England from India, my mother made it her mission to recreate the punchy flavours of the spiced snacks from Delhi street stalls. Although we lived in a rural village, she managed to bring all the fun of a South Asian marketplace to our family kitchen in northern England.

SERVES 4 AS A SIDE SALAD

500g small new potatoes, unpeeled
juice of 1 lime
1 red onion, diced
1/2 tsp cracked black peppercorns
1 green chilli, seeded and finely chopped
2 tbsp chopped fresh coriander (cilantro),
    plus extra to garnish

CHUTNEY:
150g tamarind
125g (3/4 cup) chopped, stoned dates
175g (1 1/4 cups) jaggery or light muscovado sugar
1 tsp ground ginger
1/4 tsp garam masala
2 tsp cumin seeds, toasted and ground

1 To make the chutney, break up the tamarind and put it in a pan with the dates and jaggery. Pour over enough water to cover, about 500ml (scant 2 1/4 cups), and bring to the boil. Reduce the heat and simmer for about 20 minutes, until the tamarind and dates are really soft.

2 Remove the pan from the heat and leave to cool. Press the chutney through a wire sieve (strainer) to remove the seeds and fibres.

3 Stir in the ground ginger, garam masala, and half of the cumin powder. Taste the chutney adding a touch more jaggery, if needed. Pour in a dash of water if it is too thick – aim for a coating consistency. Chill well before serving.

4 Boil the potatoes until tender. Halve each one and tip into a large mixing bowl. Combine the lime juice, red onion, cracked peppercorns, green chilli, fresh coriander (cilantro), and the remaining cumin powder. Pour the dressing over the warm potatoes and leave on one side to cool.

5 Drizzle the tamarind and date chutney over the salad and garnish with more chopped coriander (cilantro) before serving.

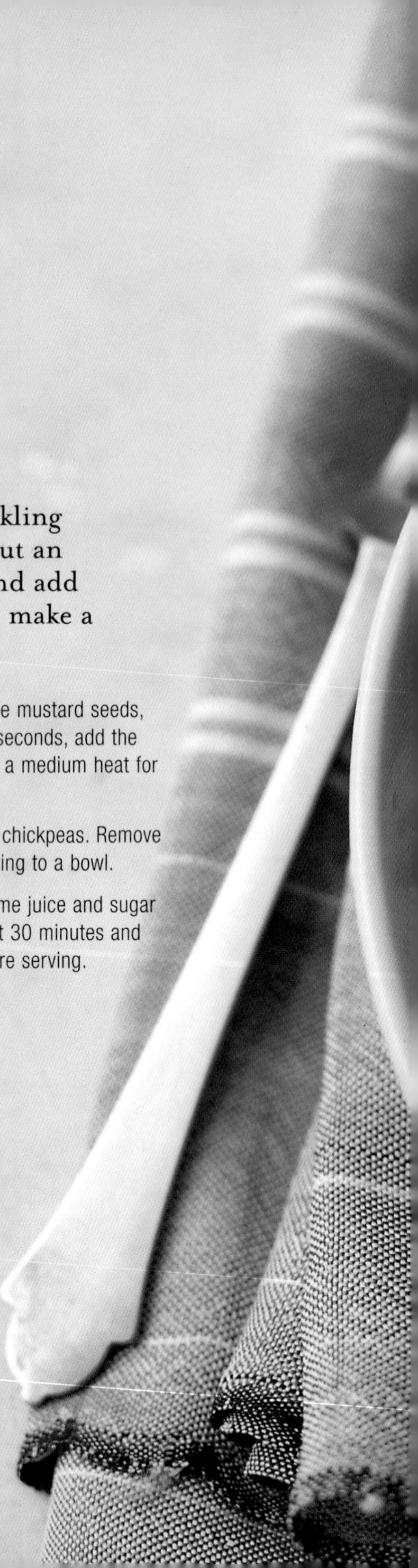

pineapple and chickpea salad

A salad crammed with tropical, sun-kissed ingredients: crackling curry leaves, fiery chillies, and toasted mustard seeds send out an enticing aroma as they sizzle in the pan. Ring the changes and add these fried spices to a regular French dressing next time you make a salad — it's that simple.

SERVES 4

30ml (2 tbsp) vegetable oil
1 tsp mustard seeds
$^1/_2$ tsp chilli flakes
1 tbsp curry leaves, shredded
$^1/_2$ tsp cracked black peppercorns
300g (2 cups) fresh pineapple pieces
400g (14oz) can chickpeas, drained and rinsed
2 tbsp grated fresh coconut
juice of 2 limes
1–2 tsp sugar
2 sprigs fresh coriander (cilantro), to garnish

1 Heat the oil in a large pan and toss in the mustard seeds, chilli flakes, and curry leaves. After a few seconds, add the cracked peppercorns and fry, stirring, over a medium heat for about 30 seconds.

2 Stir in the pineapple pieces and add the chickpeas. Remove the pan from the heat and transfer everything to a bowl.

3 Sprinkle over the coconut and add the lime juice and sugar to taste. Leave the salad to steep for about 30 minutes and garnish with fresh coriander (cilantro) before serving.

sweet mango chutney

Simple to make and packed with fruity flavour — this chunky chutney is a class apart from shop-bought varieties. For best results, buy the mangoes from a specialist grocer and don't be afraid to give them a squeeze — steer clear of any that feel even slightly squishy, the firmer the better.

MAKES 800ML (3¼ CUPS)

1kg (2lb 4oz) firm green mangoes
1 tsp turmeric
1 tsp salt
30ml (2 tbsp) vegetable oil
¾ tsp nigella seeds
1 tsp fennel seeds
½ tsp chilli flakes
4cm (1½in) fresh root ginger, peeled and chopped
200g (scant 1 cup) jaggery or light muscovado sugar

1 Peel the mangoes, remove the central stones and cut the fruit into 3cm (1¼in) chunks. Combine the mangoes with the turmeric and salt.

2 Heat the oil in a medium saucepan and toss in the nigella, fennel seeds, and chilli flakes.

3 After about 30 seconds, add the mangoes and fry over a medium heat for 5 minutes. Pour in 500ml (2 cups) water and simmer until the fruit has softened and cooked down.

4 Stir in the jaggery or sugar and cook over a moderate heat for a further 15 minutes, until the chutney has thickened. To test for setting point, spoon a teaspoonful of hot chutney onto a chilled plate then return the plate to the fridge for a minute — the surface should wrinkle when you push a finger through it.

5 When the chutney has cooled, spoon it into sterilised jars and seal tightly. It should keep for about 2–3 months; refrigerate after opening.

tomato chutney

This bold, gingery chutney is so moreish that I like to use it as a base of a meal: for a quick on-the-go lunch, serve it warm with a heap of fluffy rice, halved hard-boiled eggs, and a sprinkling of chopped coriander (cilantro) before bringing to the table.

MAKES 500ML (2 CUPS)

45ml (3 tbsp) vegetable oil
2 tsp mustard seeds
½ tsp nigella seeds
1 tbsp fennel seeds
2 red onions, diced
2 garlic cloves, finely chopped
3cm (1¼in) fresh root ginger, peeled and finely chopped
2 large green chillies, seeded and chopped
2 x 400g (14oz) cans chopped tomatoes
100g (scant ½ cup) chopped dates
40–55g (3–4 tbsp) caster sugar
100ml (⅓ cup) white wine vinegar

1 Heat the oil in a medium saucepan set over a medium heat. Add the mustard seeds and fry for a few seconds until they stop popping. Stir in the nigella and fennel seeds, and fry for another 10 seconds.

2 Turn down the heat and add the onions, garlic, ginger, green chillies, tomatoes, dates, sugar, and vinegar. Simmer, uncovered, for 10–15 minutes, until thickened. It should have a sweet-sour taste; add more sugar if needed. Serve warm or at room temperature.

chicken

sweet and tangy chicken curry

A fabulous dish to make for a crowd: this recipe has been adopted and adapted by almost everyone in our extended family. My sister likes to add a teaspoon of fresh thyme leaves instead of the more elusive carom seeds — it works like a dream!

SERVES 4

6 chicken thighs, about 800g (1lb 12oz), skinned
75g (6 tbsp) butter
3 red onions, diced
$^3/_4$ tsp dried chilli flakes
4cm (1$^1/_2$in) fresh root ginger, peeled and grated
$^1/_2$ tsp carom seeds
$^1/_2$ tsp cumin seeds, toasted and ground
1 tsp garam masala
2 x 400g (14oz) cans chopped tomatoes
45ml (3 tbsp) white wine vinegar
3 tsp sugar
fresh coriander (cilantro), to garnish

1 Preheat the grill to its highest setting. Arrange the chicken in a grill pan. Melt the butter in a large saucepan and use part of it to brush liberally over the chicken pieces. Grill the chicken for about 5 minutes on both sides, until sealed. Keep warm while you make the curry.

2 Soften the onions in the remaining melted butter in the pan. Add the chilli flakes, ginger, carom seeds, cumin, and garam masala. Fry, stirring, for 1 minute.

3 Tip in the tomatoes, followed by the vinegar and sugar. Bring to simmering point and add the chicken pieces. Cook, uncovered, for about 20 minutes, until the chicken is cooked through and the tomato sauce has reduced and thickened. (The sauce should be sweet with a pleasant tang — add more sugar or vinegar as necessary.) Garnish with fresh coriander (cilantro).

(Pictured previous page.)

home-style chicken curry

This dish takes me back to my childhood when my mother began cooking the evening meal by prising the lid off the spice box and choosing spices with as much care as others might select cosmetic colours. It's a curry that has her personality stamped all over it.

SERVES 4

90ml (6 tbsp) vegetable oil
1$^1/_2$ tsp cumin seeds
8 green cardamom pods
2 dried bay leaves
$^1/_2$ tsp black peppercorns
2 red onions, finely chopped
3 green chillies, split, seeded, and shredded
6 ripe tomatoes, skinned, seeded, and finely chopped
2 tsp tomato purée
4cm (1$^1/_2$in) fresh root ginger, peeled and shredded
6 garlic cloves, finely chopped
6 chicken thighs, 800g (1lb 12oz), skinned
$^1/_2$ tsp turmeric
$^1/_2$ tsp chilli powder
1 tsp garam masala
1 tbsp chopped fresh coriander (cilantro) stems

1 Heat the oil in a sturdy casserole pan or wok set over a moderate heat. Toss in the cumin seeds, cardamom pods, bay leaves, and peppercorns. Swirl the spices around in the oil for about 30 seconds, until they give off a lovely nutty aroma.

2 Tip in the onions and green chillies. Turn the heat to low and fry for 5–10 minutes, until the onions are just beginning to colour.

3 Stir in the tomatoes and purée followed by the ginger and garlic. Cook for another 5 minutes.

4 Turn the heat to medium and add the chicken, turmeric, chilli powder, and garam masala. Continue frying, stirring all the time, for about 10 minutes, until the onion mixture darkens and the chicken is half-cooked.

5 Pour in 250ml (1 cup) hot water, turn the heat to low and simmer for 15 minutes, uncovered, until the chicken is tender. Scatter with coriander (cilantro) stems before serving.

chicken korma

A true korma has little to do with western-inspired cook-in sauces. It's a showcase for aromatic spice combinations, silken pastes, and marvellously rich masalas. Here's a recipe I surreptitiously jotted down while working with a former royal chef — it's the ultimate party dish. Swap the cream for yoghurt if you fancy a lighter note.

1 Finely slice 2 of the onions. Sprinkle them liberally with salt and leave on one side for around 30 minutes. Squeeze out any excess water from the onions and pat them dry with kitchen towels.

2 Heat the oil for deep-frying in a deep pan or wok and fry the sliced onions in batches. When they turn golden, remove them from the oil with a slotted spoon and drain on kitchen towels.

3 Tip the fried onions into a food processor and pour in 75ml (5 tbsp) hot water then process to a smooth paste. (This will be added to the curry later on.)

4 Cover the cashews and almonds with warm water and leave to soak for 15 minutes. Tip the nuts into a food processor and pour in about 45ml (3 tbsp) of the soaking liquid. Purée until a smooth paste then leave on one side.

5 Soak the saffron strands in 45ml (3 tbsp) warm water and set aside for 30 minutes, until the liquid turns a deep auburn.

6 Now you can start making the main curry base: dice the 2 remaining onions. Heat 6 tbsp (90ml) oil in a wok or heavy-based pan and soften the diced onions for 10 minutes. Stir in the cloves, cardamom pods, and cinnamon sticks.

7 Add the chicken thighs to the wok or pan followed by the browned onion paste, ground nuts, garlic, ginger, chilli powder, and ground coriander. Turn up the heat a little and continue frying for 10 minutes.

8 Pour in 150ml (²/₃ cup) hot water and simmer, half covered, for about 15 minutes, until the thighs are cooked through.

9 Stir in the saffron, the soaking liquid, and cream. Reheat then sprinkle with garam masala and toasted cashew nuts before serving.

SERVES 4

4 onions
6 tbsp vegetable oil, plus extra for deep frying
25g (¹/₄ cup) cashew nuts
25g (¹/₄ cup) almonds, blanched
¹/₄ tsp saffron strands
¹/₂ tsp cloves ·
10 green cardamom pods
5 brown cardamom pods
2 x 4cm (1¹/₂in) cinnamon sticks
6 chicken thighs, about 800g (1lb 12oz), skinned
4 garlic cloves, finely chopped
4cm (1¹/₂cm) fresh root ginger, peeled and finely grated
¹/₂ tsp chilli powder
1 tsp ground coriander seeds
100ml (¹/₃ cup) double (heavy) cream
¹/₂ tsp garam masala
6–8 toasted cashew nuts, chopped, to garnish
salt

saffron and cardamom chicken tikka

Besides adding a tropical flavour, fresh pineapple contains an enzyme that acts as a natural meat tenderiser and also helps to cut down on cooking time. These delectable morsels have a deliciously smoky wisp of a crust and make marvellous cocktail snacks.

SERVES 4

1/2 tsp saffron strands
1 tsp cardamom seeds
125ml (1/2 cup) Greek (strained plain) yoghurt
30ml (2 tbsp) thick double (heavy) cream
4cm (1 1/2 in) fresh root ginger, peeled and finely grated
1 tbsp ground almonds
125g (1 cup) fresh pineapple chunks
600g (1lb 5oz) boneless chicken thighs, skinned
    and cut into 3cm (1 1/4 in) cubes
15ml (1 tbsp) melted butter
juice of 1 lime
wedges of lime and sprigs of fresh coriander (cilantro),
    to garnish

1 Put the saffron in a small bowl with 15ml (1 tbsp) warm water. Leave to soak for 30 minutes, until the liquid turns a deep auburn.

2 Using a mortar and pestle, pound the cardamom seeds to a fine powder and whisk them into the yoghurt. Stir in the cream, ginger, and ground almonds.

3 Finely chop the pineapple or blend it to a paste in a small food processor. Using your hands, squeeze out any excess juice, and add the pulp to the spiced yoghurt.

4 Add the chicken to the yoghurt mixture. Pour over the saffron and soaking liquid, stir well, cover with plastic wrap, and leave to marinate overnight in the fridge.

5 Preheat a grill to its highest setting. Drain the chicken pieces from the yoghurt and thread them onto skewers.

6 Pour melted butter over each skewer and cook the chicken near the top of the grill for about 5 minutes on each side, until cooked through and beginning to char at the edges.

7 Sharpen with lime juice and garnish the chicken with wedges of lime and sprigs of coriander (cilantro) before serving.

Absolutely FABULOUS — rice stuffing a MUST!

whole tandoori chicken

Glistening with toasted spices, this whole roast chicken is steeped in a cloak of garlic and ginger yoghurt and filled with mint rice and sweet apricots. After the chicken is cooked, my guilty pleasure is to mop-up any juices from the roasting tin with a thick crust of white bread.

SERVES 4

1.5kg (3lb 5oz) chicken, skinned
³/₄ tsp turmeric
1 tsp chilli powder
2 tsp black peppercorns, cracked
2 tsp salt
60ml (4 tbsp) white wine vinegar
15ml (1 tbsp) vegetable oil

YOGHURT MARINADE:
150ml (²/₃ cup) Greek (strained plain) yoghurt
4cm (1¹/₂in) fresh root ginger, peeled and grated
6 garlic cloves, finely chopped
2 green chillies, finely chopped
¹/₂ tsp garam masala
¹/₂ tsp cumin seeds, toasted and ground

MINT RICE:
75g (¹/₂ cup) basmati rice
50g (4 tbsp) butter
4 green cardamom pods, split
2 spring onions (scallions), finely chopped
25g dried apricots, finely chopped
handful fresh mint leaves
1 tsp sugar

1 Put the chicken in a roasting tin and using a sharp knife make 2 slashes across the breast, thighs, and drumsticks.

2 Combine the turmeric, chilli powder, cracked peppercorns, salt, vinegar, and oil in a small bowl and use to coat the chicken on all sides. Cover loosely with plastic wrap and leave to marinate in the fridge for 30 minutes while you make the yoghurt marinade.

3 Whisk the yoghurt in a bowl until smooth then stir in the ginger, garlic, green chillies, garam masala, and cumin. Spoon this mixture over the chicken until coated and cover with plastic wrap. Leave to marinate overnight in the fridge.

4 Cook the rice in boiling salted water for about 10 minutes before draining it in a colander. Spread the grains out onto a clean tea towel and leave to cool.

5 Preheat the oven to 200°C/400°F. Melt the butter in a small saucepan set over a low heat and add the cardamom pods. After about 30 seconds, tip in the spring onions (scallions) and soften for 2–3 minutes before adding the apricots then cook for another minute.

6 Sprinkle the mint leaves with sugar and roughly chop. Add to the spring onion (scallion) and apricot mixture along with the cooled, cooked rice.

7 Pour off any excess marinade from the chicken into a small bowl. Fill the chicken cavity with the mint rice and tie the legs with string.

8 Roast the chicken in a preheated oven for about 1 hour 20 minutes, spooning over a tablespoon or so of the marinade every 20 minutes; this helps to keep the chicken succulent as it cooks. If the chicken looks like it is browning too quickly, cover loosely with foil as it roasts. Pierce a thigh with a knife, the chicken is ready when the juices run clear and there are no traces of pink.

meat

roast spiced leg of lamb

During the British Raj, cooks at many of the Indian club kitchens took to 'perking-up' Sunday roasts with the addition of spices, and it's a legacy that has lived on. Serve this succulent roast with cumin potatoes and a warm tomato and date chutney.

SERVES 6

1½ tsp fennel seeds
200ml (¾ cup) plain yoghurt
juice 1 lime
2 tsp dried mint
2 tsp ground ginger
2 tsp paprika
1 tsp garam masala
4 garlic cloves, finely chopped
2kg (4lb 8oz) leg of lamb

1 Heat a small griddle or sturdy frying pan (skillet) over a medium heat and toast the fennel seeds for about 30 seconds until aromatic. Using a mortar and pestle, pound the seeds until finely ground.

2 Combine the ground fennel with the yoghurt, lime juice, dried mint, ground ginger, paprika, garam masala, and garlic.

3 Put the lamb in a snug-fitting roasting tin (pan). Using a sharp knife, make deep slashes across the meat down to the bone. Spoon the spiced yoghurt over the lamb, working it into the cuts. Cover and leave overnight in the fridge.

4 Preheat the oven to 220°C/425°F. Pour off any excess spiced yoghurt from the roasting tin. Roast the lamb for 30 minutes before turning down the oven to 170°C/325°F; continue to cook for about 1 hour 30 minutes. The meaty juices should run clear when the lamb is pierced with a knife. If the lamb is browning too quickly, cover loosely with foil. Leave the meat to rest for 15 minutes before carving into slices.

(Pictured previous page)

lamb chops with spinach and peppercorn crust

This dish started off as another of my mother's simple suppers — the spinach and paneer topping, a smart ploy to get us kids to relish our greens.

SERVES 4

8 lamb cutlets
8cm (3in) fresh root ginger, peeled
6 garlic cloves, finely chopped
1 tsp turmeric
¾ tsp chilli flakes
45ml (3 tbsp) white wine vinegar

SPINACH AND PEPPERCORN CRUST:

15g (1 tbsp) butter
2 green chillies, seeded and finely chopped
½ tsp black peppercorns, cracked
large handful baby spinach leaves
25g (2 tbsp) grated paneer or ricotta cheese

1 Put the cutlets in a shallow dish. Finely grate half of the ginger and combine with the garlic, turmeric, chilli flakes, and vinegar. Pour the spiced vinegar over the lamb making sure it is well coated. Cover with plastic wrap and leave in the fridge for 4–6 hours, or overnight if you have the time.

2 For the crust: shred the remaining ginger. Heat the butter in a saucepan set over a medium heat. Toss in the ginger, chillies, and peppercorns. Fry for 1 minute before adding the spinach then continue to cook until the leaves have wilted. Take the pan off the heat and leave to cool slightly.

3 Preheat the grill to its highest setting. Roughly chop the spinach and combine with the paneer or ricotta cheese. Leave on one side while you start grilling the cutlets. Put the cutlets on the grill (broiler) pan and cook for about 5–7 minutes on one side. Turn the cutlets over and grill for a further minute.

4 Spread a thin layer of the spinach and cheese mixture over each lamb cutlet and pop back under the grill (broiler) for another 3–4 minutes before serving.

ginger beef curry with poppy seeds

In India, spices are pulverised on a grinding stone — all that bashing and bruising brings out an intensity of flavour. A mortar and pestle does pretty much the same job: try using it for pounding the poppy and fennel seeds for this aromatic curry — you'll never want to buy ready-ground spices again.

1 Finely shred 3cm (1¼in) of the fresh ginger. Combine the chillies with the ginger. Squeeze over the lime juice and leave to steep for an hour or so (this will be used to garnish the curry). Finely chop the remaining ginger.

2 Heat a griddle or small frying pan (skillet) over a medium heat and toast the poppy and fennel seeds for about 30 seconds, until they give off a nutty aroma. Using a mortar and pestle, pound the seeds until finely ground. Combine the ground seeds with the cinnamon, chilli powder, turmeric, garlic, and finely chopped ginger to make a paste.

3 Put the beef in a large mixing bowl and stir in the spice paste. Turn the meat until it is coated in the spices then leave to marinate.

4 Heat the oil in a sturdy casserole pan set over a medium heat. Toss in the mustard seeds followed by the curry leaves, dried chillies, and cardamom pods. Swirl everything around for about 30 seconds, until the curry leaves stop spluttering. Add the onion to the pan, turn down the heat and cook for 5 minutes, until softened.

5 Add the spice-coated beef and marinade to the pan and fry, stirring, over a medium heat until the curry becomes dry and the meat has browned. Sprinkle over the sugar and fry for another minute.

6 Pour in 300ml (1¼ cups) hot water, cover, and simmer the curry for about 45 minutes, until the meat is tender. If you prefer a thinner sauce add an extra 105ml (7 tbsp) water.

7 Scatter the lime-steeped ginger and chilli strips over the curry and sharpen with a little of the lime juice, to taste. Sprinkle with toasted sesame seeds, to garnish.

SERVES 4

7cm (2¾in) fresh root ginger, peeled
2 red chillies, seeded and cut into thin strips
juice of 1 lime
1 tbsp poppy seeds
2 tsp fennel seeds
½ tsp ground cinnamon
1 tsp chilli powder
½ tsp turmeric
6 garlic cloves, finely chopped
600g (1lb 5oz) stewing beef, cut into 3cm (1¼in) cubes
90ml (6 tbsp) vegetable oil
1 tsp mustard seeds
12 curry leaves
4 dried red chillies
6 green cardamom pods, split
1 onion, finely chopped
1 tsp dark muscovado sugar
2 tsp toasted sesame seeds, to garnish

green chilli mince

The original recipe, handwritten in a well-used notebook, has long since faded: entire sentences have been blurred by stray smudges of yoghurt and occasional splatters.

SERVES 4

125ml (¹/₂ cup) Greek (strained plain) yoghurt
1 tsp turmeric
¹/₂ tsp cumin seeds
500g (1lb 2oz) minced lamb
4 onions
90ml (6 tbsp) vegetable oil
1 small garlic bulb, peeled, cloves halved lengthways
8 large green chillies, seeded and chopped into
  1cm (¹/₂in) pieces
squeeze of lime juice

1 Mix together the yoghurt, turmeric, and cumin seeds in a large bowl. Add the mince and stir until combined. Leave on one side for 30 minutes.

2 Slice 2 of the onions and dice the remaining onions. Heat the oil in a sturdy pan – a cast iron one is perfect. Fry the sliced onions over a gentle heat until golden.

3 Turn the heat to medium, tip in the mince mixture and fry for 5 minutes. Pour over enough hot water to barely cover and add the diced onions, garlic cloves, and green chillies. Cover with a lid and simmer for 10 minutes.

4 Remove the lid and cook the mince for about 15 minutes, until the liquid has reduced and the lamb browned; add a dash of water if it begins to catch on the bottom. The mince is ready when the garlic and spices smell toasted. Add a squeeze of lime juice to sharpen.

pork vindaloo

About as far as you can get from a British-inspired curry, this Goan classic started off as a garlicky Portuguese dish and was adapted to suit local tastes. Make it a day ahead to give its tart, tangy flavours a chance to mellow and mingle.

SERVES 4

¹/₂ tsp chilli powder
1 tsp paprika
¹/₂ tsp ground cinnamon
1 tsp garam masala
¹/₂ tsp turmeric
4cm (1¹/₂in) fresh root ginger, peeled and finely chopped
4 garlic cloves, finely chopped
60ml (4 tbsp) white wine vinegar
500g (1lb 2oz) boneless pork, from the shoulder,
  cut into 3cm (1¹/₄in) cubes
60ml (4 tbsp) vegetable oil
1 star anise
1 large onion, sliced
1 tsp brown sugar

1 Mix together the chilli powder, paprika, cinnamon, garam masala, turmeric, ginger, garlic, and vinegar in a mixing bowl then add the pork. Stir to coat the pork in the spices and marinate for 2–3 hours.

2 Heat the oil in a sturdy casserole pan and toss in the star anise. Swirl it around for a few seconds before adding the onion. Turn the heat down to low, cover the pan, and fry for 5 minutes, until softened.

3 Take the lid off the pan and raise the heat to medium. Tip in the pork and marinade and fry, stirring, for about 15 minutes, until the meat has browned and most of the liquid reduced.

4 Sprinkle in the sugar and fry for another 5 minutes, adding a dash of water if the meat begins to catch on the bottom of the pan.

5 Pour in about 200ml (³/₄ cup) hot water. Cover the pan and simmer for about 45 minutes, until the pork is tender and the masala has thickened. Add a dash more water while the curry is cooking if you think it is needed; this curry has a thick, clinging spice masala.

(Pictured on page 1)

koftas in cinnamon masala

Punjabi comfort food doesn't get better than this — meatballs spiked with astringent chillies and aromatic coriander are complemented by the appealing warmth of toasted cinnamon in a spicy tomato masala. Serve with freshly boiled rice or warm Indian breads.

SERVES 4

3 onions
7cm (2³/₄in) fresh root ginger, peeled and finely chopped
2 green chillies, finely chopped
4 tbsp chopped fresh coriander (cilantro)
¹/₂ tsp ground cinnamon
500g (1lb 2oz) minced lamb
1 egg, lightly beaten
90ml (6 tbsp) vegetable oil
2 x 3cm (1³/₄in) cinnamon sticks
1 tsp turmeric
³/₄ tsp garam masala
400g (14oz) can chopped tomatoes
2 tbsp plain yoghurt

1 To make the koftas, finely dice one of the onions and 3cm (1¹/₄in) of the ginger. Mix the onion and ginger with the chillies, 3 tbsp of the fresh coriander (cilantro), ground cinnamon, and minced lamb. Mix in the egg to bind everything together.

2 Using wet hands, shape the spiced lamb into meatballs, about 3cm (1³/₄in) in diameter. Set on a tray and chill, covered, for 30 minutes.

3 Heat the oil in a large casserole pan set over a medium heat. Fry the meatballs in batches for about 3–5 minutes, until sealed and browned. Remove from the pan and set aside while you make the masala.

4 Grate the 2 remaining onions. Add the cinnamon sticks to the casserole pan and after about 30 seconds stir in the grated onions. Turn the heat down a little and soften for 5 minutes.

5 Finely grate the remaining ginger and add to the pan with the turmeric and garam masala then fry for a minute before tipping in the tomatoes. Pour in about 200ml (³/₄ cup) hot water and bring to the boil.

6 Add the meatballs to the pan along with any juices, reduce the heat and simmer for 20 minutes, until cooked through.

7 Drizzle the yoghurt over the koftas and garnish with rest of the chopped coriander (cilantro) before serving.

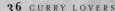

lamb biryani

True biryanis are the ultimate party dish and showcase the very best of Mughal cooking. This elegant North Indian classic combines the fragrance of basmati rice with home-ground garam masala and meltingly tender pieces of lamb.

SERVES 6-8

1/2 tsp saffron strands
3/4 tsp cardamom seeds
2 blades mace
4 onions
90ml (6 tbsp) vegetable oil, plus extra for deep frying
8cm (3 1/2 in) fresh root ginger, peeled
6 garlic cloves, finely chopped
1 tsp chilli powder
juice of 1 lime
750g (1lb 10oz) boneless lamb, from the shoulder, cut into 4cm (1 1/2 in) cubes
6 green cardamom pods
6 brown cardamom pods
5cm (2in) cinnamon stick
1/2 tsp cloves
2 dried bay leaves
1 tsp garam masala
3 green chillies, split lengthways, shredded, and seeded
200ml (3/4 cup) Greek (strained plain) yoghurt
450g (2 1/4 cups) basmati rice
handful fresh mint leaves
30g (2 tbsp) butter

1 Soak the saffron in 30ml (2 tbsp) hot water and set aside until ready to use.

2 Using a mortar and pestle, pound the cardamom seeds and mace to a powder then leave on one side; you'll need this later when layering up the rice and meat.

3 Slice 2 of the onions then sprinkle them with salt and set aside for 20 minutes. Squeeze out any excess water from the onions and pat them dry with paper towels. Deep-fry the sliced onions in hot oil until golden and drain on paper towels. Set half aside for garnishing the biryani.

4 Transfer the remaining fried onions to a food processor, pour in 45ml (3 tbsp) hot water then purée; you should have about 30ml (2 tbsp) of onion paste.

5 Finely grate half of the ginger and combine with the garlic, chilli powder, and lime juice in a large mixing bowl. Stir in the onion paste and add the lamb. Mix everything together and leave to marinate for 1 hour.

6 Dice the 2 remaining onions. Heat 90ml (6 tbsp) oil in a large casserole pan set over a medium heat and soften the diced onions for 5 minutes, without colouring.

7 Slice the remaining ginger into fine strips and set aside. Add the green and brown cardamom pods, cinnamon, cloves, and bay leaves to the pan. Fry for about 30 seconds, until you get a warm, spicy aroma.

8 Tip in the meat and its marinade and add the garam masala, green chillies, and ginger strips. Bring to simmering point and gradually add the yoghurt, a tablespoon at a time. Cover and simmer for about 45 minutes, until the lamb is tender and the masala thickened; the sauce should be well-reduced and almost clinging to the meat.

9 Cover the rice with cold water and leave to soak for 20 minutes. Ten minutes before the meat is ready, bring a large pan of salted water to the boil. Drain the rice and add to the pan then cook for 5 minutes – it should be half-cooked and still have bite to it. Drain the rice in a colander.

10 Preheat the oven to 160°C/300°F. Put half of the hot meat in the bottom of a clean casserole pan. Cover with half of the freshly boiled rice and sprinkle with half of the ground cardamom and mace spice mixture and half of the mint.

11 Top with the remaining meat and rice. Scatter over the rest of the spice mix, mint leaves, and the sliced browned onions that you fried in step 3. Dot the surface with butter and drizzle over the saffron and its soaking liquid. Cover the biryani with wet greaseproof (waxed) paper and a well-fitting lid.

12 Bake for 40 minutes, until the rice is perfumed and perfectly cooked. Gently fluff up the grains with a fork and serve straight from the pan.

fish & seafood

grilled fish tikka

Whenever we had a party in Delhi, fish tikka always came top of the wish list. Any firm white fish will suffice, and there are plenty of sustainable varieties worth checking out.

SERVES 4

1 onion, thinly sliced
vegetable oil, for deep frying
150ml (²/₃ cup) Greek (strained plain) yoghurt
juice of 1 lime
4 garlic cloves, finely chopped
4cm (1¹/₂in) fresh root ginger, peeled and grated
¹/₂ tsp cumin seeds, toasted and ground
2 tsp paprika
1 tsp mango powder
1 tbsp gram flour
100ml (scant ¹/₂ cup) thick double (heavy) cream
1 egg yolk
500g (1lb 2oz) haddock, pollack or coley fillet, skinned,
    cut into 4cm (1¹/₂in) cubes

TO GARNISH:
1 small red onion, cut into rings
1 tbsp fresh coriander (cilantro) leaves
1 lime, cut into wedges

1 Sprinkle the sliced onion with salt and set aside for 20 minutes. Squeeze out any excess water from the onion and pat dry with paper towels. Deep-fry the onion until golden then drain on paper towels.

2 Transfer the fried onion to a food processor; pour in about 45ml (3 tbsp) hot water and process until smooth. Leave the onions to cool.

3 Combine the onion paste with the yoghurt and stir in the lime juice, garlic, ginger, ground cumin, paprika, mango powder, and gram flour. Whisk in the cream and egg yolk.

4 Put the fish in a mixing bowl and spoon over the yoghurt mixture. Stir gently until combined and leave to marinate for about 30 minutes.

5 Preheat the grill (broiler) to its highest setting and when hot, remove the fish from the marinade. Thread the fish onto 8 skewers then grill (broil) for about 2–3 minutes each side, until golden and tender.

6 Transfer the skewers to a serving dish and garnish with the red onion rings, fresh coriander (cilantro), and lime wedges.

(Pictured previous page)

steamed sea bass with coconut chutney

I first tasted this dish at a Parsee celebration where individual banana leaf packages of delicately steamed fish were unwrapped at the table. Serve with basmati rice.

SERVES 4

4 x 175g sea bass fillets
juice of 2 limes
4 tbsp grated fresh coconut
4 large green chillies, roughly chopped
4 tbsp roughly chopped fresh coriander (cilantro)
2 tbsp fresh mint leaves
1 tsp cumin seeds, toasted and ground
1 tsp sugar
1 lime, cut into wedges, to garnish

1 Put the fish fillets in a shallow dish and squeeze over the juice from one of the limes.

2 Put the coconut in a food processor and add the green chillies, fresh coriander, fresh mint, cumin, sugar, and the remaining lime juice. Process the chutney until smooth adding a splash of water, if needed.

3 Tear off four large squares of foil (or use banana leaves) – large enough to wrap around each sea bass fillet. Put a fillet on each piece of foil and coat with a generous layer of the coconut chutney. Wrap the foil around the fish to make a neat parcel.

4 Steam the fish for 5–7 minutes, depending on the thickness of the fillets. Unwrap each parcel at the table and serve straight away. (Alternatively, bake the parcels at 180°C/350°F for about 15 minutes.) Garnish with wedges of lime.

keralan fish curry

The sun-kissed toasted spices, creamy coconut milk, and aromatic curry leaves in this homely curry celebrate the flavours of traditional South Indian cooking. Serve with a mound of fluffy rice and spoonfuls of a lemony pickle.

1 Combine the paprika, turmeric, and lime juice in a large mixing bowl. Add the turbot then stir to coat the fish in the marinade; leave to marinate while you make the curry base.

2 Heat a griddle or small frying pan (skillet) over a medium heat. Toast the peppercorns, coriander seeds, and fenugreek for about 1 minute, until they give off a warm, spicy aroma.

3 Using a mortar and pestle, pound the spices until they are finely ground. Add the soaked chillies and 30ml (2 tbsp) of the soaking water; continue pounding until you have a paste. Leave on one side.

4 Heat the vegetable oil in a sturdy pan set over a medium heat. Toss in the mustard seeds followed by the curry leaves. Swirl everything around for about 30 seconds then turn down the heat to low.

5 Add the onion and soften, without colouring, for 5 minutes. Stir in the spice paste, garlic, and ginger then continue to fry for 2–3 minutes.

6 Add the turbot to the pan along with any spiced lime juice and after a minute, pour in the coconut milk. Bring to a simmer and cook for about 5 minutes, until the fish is tender.

7 Scatter the cashew nuts and coconut over the curry before serving.

SERVES 4

2 tsp paprika
$3/4$ tsp turmeric
juice of 1 lime
600g (1lb 5oz) turbot or other firm white fish, cut into 4cm (1$1/2$in) cubes
1 tsp black peppercorns
1 tsp coriander seeds
$1/4$ tsp fenugreek seeds
3 dried red chillies, soaked for 20 minutes in hot water
60ml (4 tbsp) vegetable oil
1 tsp mustard seeds
2 tbsp curry leaves
1 onion, finely chopped
4 garlic cloves, shredded
4cm (1$1/2$in) fresh root ginger, peeled and shredded
250ml (1 cup) coconut milk

TO GARNISH:
1 tbsp toasted cashew nuts
1 tbsp toasted shredded coconut

bengali shrimp curry

My father is from Calcutta – the home of mustardy fish masalas. I've adapted this family recipe by adding a touch of cornflour (cornstarch) as it helps to meld everything together and works like a dream.

1 Soak the mustard seeds and dried red chillies in about 45ml (3 tbsp) hot water. Leave on one side for 30 minutes.

2 Tip the mustard seeds, dried chillies, and soaking liquid into a mortar. Add the cardamom seeds and cloves, then pound to make a slack spice paste; set aside.

3 Whisk the yoghurt in a jug until smooth. Stir in the cornflour (cornstarch), carom seeds, ground coriander, mango powder, and ground cinnamon.

4 Heat the oil in a medium-sized casserole pan. When hot, add the spice paste. Fry, stirring, for about 1 minute then pour in the spiced yoghurt. Bring to simmering point and turn the heat to low.

5 Add the prawns (shrimp) to the pan and continue to cook for 3–5 minutes, until pink. Garnish with fresh coriander (cilantro).

SERVES 4

2 tsp mustard seeds
2 dried red chillies
$\frac{1}{4}$ tsp cardamom seeds
3 cloves
250ml (1 cup) Greek (strained plain) yoghurt
$\frac{1}{2}$ tsp cornflour (cornstarch)
$\frac{1}{2}$ tsp carom seeds
2 tsp ground coriander
$1\frac{1}{2}$ tsp mango powder
$\frac{1}{4}$ tsp ground cinnamon
60ml (4 tbsp) vegetable oil
600g (1lb 5oz) uncooked king prawns (shrimp), peeled
fresh coriander (cilantro), to garnish

shrimp in tamarind sauce

I love the stickiness of this sweet-sour masala; sometimes I'll serve this dish as a cocktail snack and cook the tamarind and sugar until almost caramelised before adding the prawns (shrimp).

1 Break up the tamarind with your fingers and put it in a small heatproof bowl. Pour over 75ml (5 tbsp) boiling water and leave to steep for about 15 minutes. Once it is cool enough to handle, squeeze the pulp in your hands, discarding the seeds and fibres, and reserving the tamarind liquid. Leave on one side.

2 Heat the vegetable oil in a wok or large pan set over a medium heat. Toss in the fennel seeds, nigella, and fenugreek. Swirl the spices around for about 30 seconds before adding the garlic, ginger, and red chillies.

3 After a few seconds, pour in the tamarind liquid and add the sugar. Bring to the boil and cook the sauce until it becomes syrupy. Tip in the prawns (shrimp) and cook for about 3–5 minutes over a high heat, until pink. Garnish with fresh coriander (cilantro) and serve.

(Pictured on page 2)

SERVES 4

1 walnut-sized piece of tamarind
30ml (2 tbsp) vegetable oil
1 tsp fennel seeds
$\frac{1}{4}$ tsp nigella seeds
$\frac{1}{4}$ tsp fenugreek seeds
4 garlic cloves, finely chopped
4cm ($1\frac{1}{2}$in) fresh root ginger, peeled and finely shredded
2 red chillies, split, seeded, and shredded
2 tsp jaggery or dark muscovado sugar
500g (1lb 2oz) uncooked king prawns (shrimp), shelled
1 tbsp chopped fresh coriander (cilantro), to garnish

vegetables

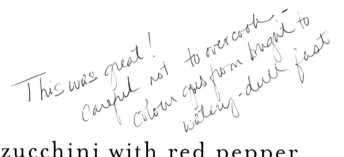

This was great! Careful not to overcook — colour goes from bright to watery-dull fast

spiced zucchini with red pepper

Delicate and subtly spiced, this courgette (zucchini) and (bell) pepper dish has a hint of Mediterranean flavour, and is a regular choice for a simple lunch. If you like more 'heat', leave the chilli seeds in.

SERVES 4

45ml (3 tbsp) vegetable oil
3 red onions, finely sliced
4cm (1½in) fresh root ginger, peeled and shredded
2 red chillies, split, seeded, and shredded
1 red (bell) pepper, seeded, roughly chopped
4 courgettes (zucchini), thinly sliced
squeeze of lemon juice
½ tsp cumin seeds, toasted and ground
2 tbsp chopped fresh coriander (cilantro)

1 Heat the oil in a sturdy casserole pan and soften the onions over a very gentle heat, stirring occasionally; it is best to cover the pan while the onions are cooking.

2 Add the ginger, chillies, and the red (bell) pepper to the pan. Continue cooking, with the lid off, for 3–5 minutes, until the onions are softened and golden.

3 Add the courgettes (zucchini) and cook for a further 5 minutes, until they are tender but still have bite. Sharpen with a squeeze of lemon juice. Sprinkle with the ground cumin and fresh coriander (cilantro).

(Pictured previous page)

potatoes with cumin

A reliable family favourite, these potatoes are the mainstay of a Punjabi picnic. Best enjoyed with gingery Chickpea Curry (see page 63) and a stack of Indian breads, the potatoes also make a marvellous match with meaty grills and Sunday roasts.

SERVES 4

60ml (4 tbsp) vegetable oil
1½ tsp cumin seeds
½ tsp turmeric
½ tsp chilli powder
4cm (1½in) fresh root ginger, peeled and finely chopped
600g (1lb 5oz) new potatoes, peeled and cut into 1cm (½in) dice

1 Heat the oil in a sturdy frying pan, with a lid, set over a medium heat. Toss in the cumin seeds and swirl around in the oil for 30 seconds, until they have darkened. Turn the heat to low, add the turmeric, chilli powder, and ginger then fry for a further 30 seconds.

2 Add the diced potatoes, stir well to coat them in the spices and cover the pan. Cook over a very low heat for about 15 minutes, until the potatoes are cooked. Stir once or twice during cooking to make sure the potatoes do not catch on the bottom of the pan. Serve warm as an accompaniment.

stir-fried okra

When fried until crisp, okra takes on a deliciously nutty flavour, and is sharpened with the tang of dried mango powder and red chillies. You can add a sweet-sour note by including freshly grated coconut and a touch of brown sugar to the filling.

SERVES 4

500g (1lb 2oz) okra
4 tsp mango powder
2 tsp chilli powder
1 tsp turmeric
1 tsp salt
60ml (4 tbsp) vegetable oil

1 Cut the tops off the okra and make an incision along the length of each one to make a pocket to fill with the spices.

2 Combine the mango powder, chilli powder, turmeric, and salt. Using a teaspoon, sprinkle $1/2$ tsp of the mixed spices inside the okra. (You will have some spice mixture leftover for future use.)

3 Heat the oil in a sturdy frying pan set over a low heat. Fry the okra for about 15 minutes, until they darken and become crisp. Drain on paper towels and serve as a side dish, accompanied with flat bread.

cabbage thoran

Valued for their robust flavour, curry leaves are the salt and pepper seasoning of South Indian cooking. When fried in hot oil, they crackle and give off an appealing citrus aroma, laced with shades of smokiness. I buy the fresh leaves from Asian grocers and freeze any surplus in plastic bags.

SERVES 4

30ml (2 tbsp) vegetable oil
2 tsp mustard seeds
1 tbsp curry leaves
2 tsp dried chilli flakes
2 small red onions, sliced
4cm ($1^1/_2$in) fresh root ginger, peeled and finely shredded
4 small new potatoes, unpeeled
$^1/_2$ tsp turmeric
1 small Savoy cabbage, finely sliced
2 tomatoes, diced
2 tbsp grated fresh coconut

1 Heat the oil in a large wok or saucepan set over a medium heat. Toss in the mustard seeds, followed by the curry leaves and chilli flakes. Swirl everything around until the leaves stop spluttering.

2 Turn the heat to low then tip in the onions and ginger then soften for 5 minutes.

3 While the onions are cooking, thinly slice the potatoes and add to the pan with the turmeric. Stir well to coat the potatoes in the spices, cover the pan, and cook for about 10 minutes over a gentle heat, until tender.

4 Tip in the cabbage, mix everything together, and fry for another 10 minutes, until softened.

5 Stir in the tomatoes and sprinkle with coconut before serving.

(Pictured on page 5)

paneer and creamy spinach curry

The simple seasoning of fried garlic, ginger, and chilli in this creamy spinach dish makes it particularly memorable. Serve with a stack of hot buttery breads.

SERVES 4

60ml (4 tbsp) vegetable oil
1 tsp cumin seeds
1 tsp chilli flakes
6 garlic cloves, chopped
4cm (1½in) fresh root ginger, peeled and chopped
750g (1lb 10oz) baby spinach leaves
½ tsp garam masala
120ml (½ cup) single (light) cream
200g (scant 2 cups) firm paneer, cut into 2cm (¾in) cubes

1 Heat the vegetable oil in a large pan set over a medium heat. Toss in the cumin seeds and chilli flakes then swirl them around in the oil for about 30 seconds.

2 Turn down the heat to low, add the garlic and ginger, and continue to cook for another few seconds. Tip the spinach into the pan, sprinkle in the garam masala, and stir to combine. Cook, uncovered, over a medium heat for about 8–10 minutes, until the leaves have cooked down and become really soft. Leave to cool.

3 Tip the leaves, along with any juices from the pan, into a food processor and blend until smooth (you could also finely chop the leaves). Return the puréed spinach to the pan, reheat, then pour in the cream. Just before serving, add the cubed paneer and warm through.

watermelon curry with mint

Fresh and invigorating, this fruity curry is as healthy as it is tasty. Spiked with chilli and sweetened with toasted fennel seeds, it's best served with a mound of white rice.

SERVES 4

½ small watermelon, about 2kg (4lb 8oz)
1 tsp paprika
¼ tsp turmeric
½ tsp dried mint
½ tsp garam masala
1 green chilli, seeded and chopped
3cm (1¼in) fresh root ginger, peeled and chopped
30ml (2 tbsp) vegetable oil
2 tsp fennel seeds
juice of ½ lime
1 tbsp shredded fresh mint leaves

1 Cut the skin and pith away from the watermelon, remove any seeds, and roughly cube the flesh.

2 Put half of the watermelon in an electric blender and add the paprika, turmeric, dried mint, garam masala, green chilli, and ginger. Process until smooth and set aside.

3 Heat the oil in a wok or large saucepan set over a medium heat. Toss in the fennel seeds and swirl around in the oil for a few seconds until they darken. Add the spiced watermelon purée. Bring to a boil and cook for about 10 minutes until it becomes syrupy.

4 Add the remaining watermelon cubes to the hot sauce and warm through. Sharpen with lime juice and scatter over the shredded mint.

pulses & lentils

makhani dal

The ultimate party dish, this creamy, dark-hued dal is a northern classic and a popular choice at Punjabi feasts.

SERVES 4

150g (scant ¾ cup) urad dal, black lentils
75g (scant ⅓ cup) chana dal, yellow split peas
50g (¼ cup) dried red kidney beans
1 bulb garlic, cloves separated and peeled
6cm (2½in) fresh root ginger, peeled and roughly chopped
4 green chillies
60ml (4 tbsp) tomato purée
75g (6 tbsp) unsalted butter
125ml (½ cup) double (heavy) cream

1 Combine the dried lentils, peas, and red kidney beans in a large bowl. Cover with cold water and leave to soak overnight. The next morning, discard the soaking water, rinse the lentil mixture and transfer it to a sturdy casserole pan.

2 Take a piece of muslin, about the size of a large handkerchief, and lay it out on the kitchen work top. Put the garlic and ginger in the centre of the muslin and make a bundle, securing the cloth with string. Add the muslin bag to the lentil mixture along with the green chillies.

3 Pour enough water into the pan to cover the lentil mixture by 4cm (1½in). Bring to the boil, then reduce the heat and simmer, half-covered, for about 2 hours, until the liquid has reduced and the pulses are soft; you may need to top up the water now and again. (If you have a pressure cooker, the beans and lentils will take about 30 minutes.)

4 Squeeze any garlic and ginger juices from the bag into the dal and discard the bag. Stir in the tomato purée, butter, and cream then reheat. This dal tastes even better made the day before serving.
(Pictured previous page)

tarka dal QUITE HOT! — not so much after "aging" very good

In India, most homes have a pot of lentils ready to serve at daily meals. This one has a particularly robust, almost nutty quality that marries well with the fried masala.

SERVES 4

200g (scant 1 cup) chana dal, yellow split peas
6cm (2½in) fresh root ginger, peeled
½ tsp turmeric
45ml (3 tbsp) vegetable oil
1½ tsp cumin seeds
1 tsp chilli flakes
1 small red onion, sliced
2 garlic cloves, chopped
1 tomato, chopped
½ tsp garam masala
2 tbsp chopped fresh coriander (cilantro)

1 Put the lentils in a sturdy casserole pan. Pour in 500ml (2¼ cups) water then add the turmeric and half of the peeled ginger; do not add any salt as it toughens the lentils.

2 Bring to the boil, then reduce the heat and simmer until the lentils are soft and breaking up. If you prefer a smooth dal, discard the chunk of ginger, leave the lentils to cool, and liquidise in an electric blender. Add a splash more water if you feel the lentils need it.

3 Finely chop the remaining ginger and set aside. Heat the oil in a small frying pan and toss in the cumin seeds followed by the chilli flakes. Swirl them around for about 20 seconds until they darken.

4 Add the onion to the pan and fry until golden. Stir in the ginger and garlic and cook for another minute. Now, add the tomato and garam masala and fry for another 2–3 minutes.

5 Tip the onion mixture into the hot dal and add the fresh coriander (cilantro); stir well before serving.

I added a touch of salt
my dal got murky in colour I wonder if white onions might keep it "yellower"

south indian-style khichri

Almost every Indian family has a favourite recipe for khichri, from soupy pick-me-ups in North India to festive Bengali feasts, and even British-inspired kedgerees. This South Indian version, topped with a gingery tomato sauce, is my favourite.

1 Dice 2 of the onions. Heat 45ml (3 tbsp) of the oil in a medium saucepan and when hot, toss in the mustard seeds followed by the curry leaves. Once the leaves stop spluttering, turn the heat down and add the onions and half of the ginger. Fry the onions for 5–10 minutes, until they soften without colouring.

2 Stir in the turmeric and chilli powder then fry for a few more seconds. Tip in the puréed tomatoes – if they are not as ripe as you would like, bolster the flavour with the tomato purée. Stir in the sugar and simmer, without a lid, for 10–15 minutes, until thickened.

3 Add the fresh coriander (cilantro) and set aside. (This sauce can be made ahead of time and reheated when you need it.)

4 To make the khichri, combine the rice and lentils in a bowl. Cover with cold water and leave to soak for 15 minutes.

5 Slice the 2 remaining onions. Heat 60ml (4 tbsp) of oil in a large pan and add the onions, the remaining ginger, and green chillies. Turn the heat down to low and cook for about 10 minutes, until softened.

6 Drain the rice and lentils and add to the sliced onions; fry, stirring, for 1 minute.

7 Pour 550ml (2¼ cups) of boiling water into the pan and simmer, uncovered, for about 10 minutes, until the rice is cooked and the lentils are tender. By now the cooking liquid should have been absorbed. Serve with the warm tomato sauce.

SERVES 4

4 red onions
105ml (7 tbsp) vegetable oil
³/₄ tsp mustard seeds
1 tbsp curry leaves
7cm (2³/₄in) fresh root ginger, peeled and finely chopped
¹/₂ tsp turmeric
¹/₂ tsp chilli powder
500g (1lb 2oz) tomatoes, skinned, seeded, and puréed
1 tsp tomato purée, optional
pinch of sugar
2 tbsp chopped fresh coriander (cilantro) leaves

KHICHRI:
250g (1¹/₄ cups) basmati rice
125g (generous ¹/₂ cup) red lentils, masoor
3 whole green chillies

rajma

This is one of the few recipes where canned beans don't deliver the fullness of flavour you get from dried pulses. Serve the beans with rice and wedges of lemon on the side.

SERVES 4

250g (generous 1¼ cups) dried red kidney beans,
  soaked overnight in water
60ml (4 tbsp) vegetable oil
2 onions, diced
4cm (1½in) fresh root ginger, peeled and finely chopped
2 green chillies, split lengthways, seeded, and shredded
4 tomatoes, skinned, seeded, and puréed
2 tsp tomato purée
¾ tsp garam masala
30ml (2 tbsp) Greek (strained plain) yoghurt
juice of 1 lime

1 Drain the water from the soaked beans and discard. Rinse the beans then tip them into a large saucepan, cover with about 1.5 litres (6¼ cups) water. Bring to the boil and cook for 1–2 hours until tender. (If using a pressure cooker, the beans should be ready in 30 minutes). Drain, saving the cooking liquor for adding to the masala later on.

2 Heat the oil in a large pan and fry the onions until golden. Stir in the ginger and green chillies and continue frying for 1–2 minutes.

3 Add the tomatoes and tomato purée to the pan and fry until the masala darkens and becomes paste-like in consistency.

4 Whisk the garam masala into the yoghurt and gradually add to the pan while it is still on the heat; continue frying for a further minute.

5 Add the cooked beans to the curry and pour in enough of the cooking liquor to make a thick sauce. Sharpen with lime juice. This curry tastes even better made the day before serving.

chickpea curry

As children we always knew when there were chickpeas for dinner from the hissing and spluttering noise from the pressure cooker — this is my mother's classic recipe.

SERVES 4

60ml (4 tbsp) vegetable oil
1 large onion, diced
4cm (1^1/$_2$in) fresh root ginger, peeled and finely chopped
^{3}/$_4$ tsp turmeric
^{1}/$_2$ tsp garam masala
^{1}/$_2$ tsp chilli powder
300g (10^1/$_2$oz) ripe tomatoes, skinned, seeded, and chopped
1 tsp tomato purée, optional
400g (14oz) can chickpeas, drained and rinsed
2 tsp ground pomegranate powder

TO GARNISH:
1 small red onion, finely diced
2 green chillies, seeded and finely shredded
juice of 2 limes

1 Heat the oil in a large saucepan over a low heat. Add the onion and ginger and soften, without colouring, for 5 minutes.

2 Turn up the heat a tad and fry until the onion becomes golden at the edges. Stir in the turmeric, garam masala, and chilli powder. Fry for another 30 seconds to cook the spices.

3 Add the tomatoes — if they are not as ripe as you would like, bolster the flavour with the tomato purée. Fry the masala, stirring all the time, for about 10 minutes, until it has darkened and thickened.

4 Stir in the chickpeas, pomegranate powder and about 150ml (^{2}/$_3$ cup) hot water. Simmer the curry for 10 minutes before serving.

5 Combine the onion, chillies, and lime juice and leave for 30 minutes. Spoon the onion mixture and a little of the lime juice over the chickpeas.

acknowledgements

This book owes much to my late mother, who filled our home with fabulous food and from whom I inherited a passion for cooking and Indian food.

I must thank Jacqui Small for her enthusiasm in commissioning *Curry Lovers*. Nicola Graimes – many thanks for your meticulous editing, and for answering late night e-mail on Sundays! I am so grateful to Richard Jung, for his perfectly proportioned images – he's an outstanding photographer. Bringing all the flavours together is the expertise of food stylist Jayne Cross – she's the best. Thanks also to Ashley Western, for shaping the pages into this visual feast.

Finally, here's to my agent Sarah Dalkin, my colleagues and friends at UKTV, and my family (especially Dan) for being so supportive, and such willing food tasters.